SAPLINGS

Snapshots of a Season
Never Meant to Last

by Amanda Calabro

Interior formatting by Asya Blue Design
Edited by Ariel So

ISBN 978-1-7375094-0-0 (paperback)
ISBN 978-1-7375094-1-7 (eBook)

to everyone who has loved and lost

to everyone who has come and gone

and most importantly—
to the twenty who laughed with me
and cried with me
and loved me for those eleven weeks
and then forever

"if we can't all eat at one table together
I'd rather eat inside a Walmart."

—s. s. m.

"there's always more room on a sectional."

—r. l.

ARRIVING

we arrived here as strangers —
some, to this place and, most,
to each other

THINGS YOU LEARN
FROM ARRIVING

I'm standing wild-eyed; my wet hair drips. My feet cling numbly to rough black shingles, and I inch my way by half steps. I look back over my exposed shoulder, goosebumps emerging from some chill deep inside myself. The small outward-opening window now snapped shut and locked, only one way down. I hear an influx of bleary voices, my brain frantic with adrenaline, trying to make sense of the fragments of encouragement that drift up from below. Tiff is beside me, a small block of fearlessness and daredevil, not a note of fear comes off her. I shift my focus back to the horizon and inch step by step until I'm a foot or less from the edge.

One floor below me is the store, a floor below that is the belly of the boathouse, and at the base are two boat slips fed from the slow laps of the lake. The slips are deep, deep enough to ensure I don't break upon submersion. But between them, planks of wood top patches of dock. From up here, even a centimeter give left or right, and my femur snaps. I line myself up with the opening twenty times to make sure it's right.

I'm not sure how I ended up here, peer pressure mixed with the small bits of thrill-seeker inside me. Maybe it's just because I can be here. There was an opportunity, a window, in this case an actual window I had to snake my body through, and I took it.

It's early summer, and the days haven't reached their peak

yet. The sun is slowly beginning its descent and flirts with treetops across the lake. It's beautiful up here. Different from the view I'm used to two stories below. The air is a battle between the warmth of the day and the chill that the impending night will bring. I don't know how many seconds or minutes or hours are passing as I stand here. My right leg is trembling, probably visibly.

Lindsay's voice breaks through the indecipherable murmurs, and I spot her in the cluster of friends that stand on main dock, two slips to my left. "The longer you look at it, the scarier it's gonna get. You just gotta do it." She's matter-of-fact. And I know she's right. Count it down, my voice shakes. From below, "one, two, three. . ."

On three I step my left foot to the edge, toes hang off, knees bend—I leap and am in freefall. I'm falling long enough to just register I'm still in the air before my body breaks the calm water. I plummet far beneath the surface into the black, deep water until the downward movement is stopped in the friction of the water and I begin to kick my way towards the surface, a smile breaking, and sweetly pure lake water slipping in between parted lips.

And that's what this summer is. It's jumping off the boat-house roof and freefalling until I break through some kind of surface, finding some kind of truth within its depths, and surfacing again better for it. And right now, here in early May, I'm standing tremble-footed at the very edge of sure safety, and a voice calls out telling me to jump. It'll be worse the longer I wait.

TO FILL

I started this journey alone
but in two-hundred hours you'd make this house a home

the barren space would soon be filled
and sooner still my heart would spill

because home is more than bone and skin
it's the soul that fills it from within

WELCOME HOME

arriving first
gave me the rarest
and greatest gift

and that was welcoming
you all
home

COMING DAYS

we didn't yet know all that we'd soon find out
and how could you blame us
when we'd only just arrived

THE RESIDENCE

who knew this
teeny
tiny
house built for five
is where
all twenty-one of us
would reside?

IN THE BEGINNING

tell me about the hardest parts
the things that make this real
tell me about where you've failed
and where you've learned to heal
with sincere words and face unveiled
be raw in every way
open bones till marrow comes
until night turns into day

BEFORE WE'VE BROKEN OPEN

it's funny
really
the way we are at the start,
picture-perfect us
so fearful
of heart

NEW

it was new
all of you
and I forgot what fear looked like

I felt like me
and now I see
it's because of who you are

ASPHALT

the roads here weren't built for us, they curve and bend and give into the delineations of the land, submissive to the forests they inhabit, and there's nothing more beautiful than that which is man-made taking its cues from that which was Created

AFTER RAIN

after rain when the sky is drained
and there is nothing left to say—

people emerge all on the verge
of something simple and great—

new buds rise and strengthen their ties
and find roots in the soil of the earth—

stillness falls and birds let out calls
and all is calm in the wake of the storm—

THE UNCERTAINTY

what am I doing here?
why did I come?

who are these strangers?
where are they from?

what will I find in them?
will they let me grow?

is it too late to turn back now?
is it too late to go?

A GUN CHOICE

standing in the summer sun
I know this journey's just begun
the choice is mine, but I must make one
look down the barrel or unload the gun

SPLIT TUNES

how can a heart beat to two different drums?
are the pieces worth more than their sum?
it's torn down the middle, half fear and half praise
with ventricles beating different tunes each day

K B
——

my safety net in a world unknown
from one summer to the next who could've known

I'm thankful for your familiar face
and for the extension you've given of grace

I seek solace in the history we share
and that alone lessens my fear

CITRUS SKIES

in the stillest moments
citrus skies reflect on
the surface of blue gray water
sun slants low and
falls behind pines
across Pelky Bay

CADENCE

there are no existing rhythms here
the cadence of this whole summer hangs
in these beginning moments

GROWING

the more we lived and leaned

the more we learned and gleaned

THINGS YOU LEARN
FROM GROWING

It's midsummer, and we're settled into our roles. Any question of process was long since answered, and any fear of leaving had yet to set in. These are the glory days suspended in eternal tension. It's Sunday night; it's after nine. We trickle our way back into the kitchen, thankfully the pit crew has gone back to their cabins for the night. This place is all ours. Sam or someone rushes out the sound booth and logs in, finding something to soundtrack the night. In the kitchen someone turns up the speaker. Tiffany goes to the rat room—the biggest misnomer, since the room is rodent proof—and grabs boxes. After returning the boxes to the table, she and the others begin assembling. Alex goes to the front table and starts delegating tasks to Nate and Jim who are told to grab the sodas from the walk-in and group them based on cabin sizes. Jake and Eli are unscrewing the lids off metallic bags filled with metallic cheese sauce, and Becca is leading the charge on salting the pretzels. She wheels the rolling rack from the walk-in, and Walker and Matt use the spray nozzle that fills the tilt skillet to soak the pretzels before sprinkling them with salt. Lindsay is gathering the last of the paper products; she and Kelsey join me around the metal cart as we dole out the correct number of plates and cups for each cabin.

Rachel's been working the ovens, loading them with soggy pretzel bites and ten minutes later pulling out golden perfection.

Suddenly the song switches to "Africa" by Toto, and I know at some point Brennan snuck out from the kitchen and added it to the Spotify queue. Maryn and Kat help the boys fill paper cups with cheese sauce and load trays of it into the warming oven. Once everything is baked off, we start loading boxes with handfuls of pretzels and containers of cheese. An assembly line forms, and everyone finds their place. The music is loud, and we sing even louder and not a word of who does what is uttered. We slide seamlessly into our roles here, anticipating peoples' next moves, knowing what needs to be done and doing it without being told or asked.

We laugh and joke and sing. My voice is coarse in my throat, but I insist on singing louder, louder, louder. I know I'll be dragging when my alarm goes off at 5:30 a.m. tomorrow, but I wouldn't miss this. We know it's almost go time when Preston and Sarah come in through the back door, their presence alerted to us by the sound of the fly fan over the door. If they're done working the sound booth and wielding the camera, it must mean campers are back in their cabins, no doubt fighting for first shower—mud staining the carpet and swirling down the drains already clogged with hair and dirt.

Sarah is still behind the lens, capturing it. Jim and Nate put Kelsey inside a rolling rack and push her around the kitchen in unsteady circles. Sarah is sitting on a cart, and Sam is racing Jim and Nate, the wheels locking in their tracks and almost sending her tipping over. Kat and Walker are dancing and somehow Alex has managed to keep everything on track despite the uproar around her. Soon the first male leaders trickle in, shouting their cabin names over the thrum of the bass. Alex and others gather behind the service table, some with me by the metal cart that holds all the cabin names with their paper goods. We race each other to find the right cabin first. I always lose to Jim.

After all the cabin leaders have come and gone, we lug in wooden chairs from the Captain's Table and circle them around the bakery table in back. We bring liter bottles of off-brand root beer and fill cups while some load up cups of cheese and extra boxes of pretzels. We're all sitting now, knee to knee, elbows bumping and stuffing our faces with unordinary amounts of salted dough. Infirmary hours must be over because Kelsie and Schuyler arrive soon after and join the feast, taking refuge in the last two empty seats around the table, radios set in front of their plates in case of an emergency call. A toast, we raise our cups, thumbs on the rim, pinkies below, creating some sort of claw grip.

It's a short affair, the eating after the work. As the clock nears eleven, we lick the last bits of salt off our fingers and throw away our plates. We return the chairs to the dining hall, then turn the music and the lights off. We wander back through darkness to the Residence, arms linked, laughing, making fun of each other like siblings. Twenty-one wild siblings. The door to the Residence creaks and squeaks, and we all kick off shoes in the foyer. Some take places on the couch, and others slink right into their beds, under cover till early morning alarms signal the start of Monday, camp Day 2.

And that's what it's like to grow. Not only farther ahead but closer together. We grow into our roles, into our jobs, into each other. We wrap and fold into one another like vines twisting around each other and together growing toward the sky. We rely on each other for strength and encouragement, a silent nod, a hug, a dance-off, some well-directed humor. We count on each other. We couldn't do it alone. Alex couldn't run ovens while arranging numbers and cabin counts. Rachel couldn't assemble paper products while cycling pretzels through the Blodgett's. We needed one another. We did it because all of our hands were in it. And this summer is just Pretzel night (p-night) expanded, blown up. We make this thing run because we can count on each other doing our jobs and being joyful through it all. Because we can count on coming home at the end of a hard day to find these friends piled around the living room waiting for you so you can take out a boat, or play a game of volleyball on the sand courts after the waterfront is closed. We have rhythm and routine, and we've settled in. Every day is different, sure, but its undercurrent is bolstered by rhythms.

There's no one else I'd rather ride this current with. We're halfway now. And I take refuge in this taught limbo I'm hanging in. Wishing I could hang in this moment forever.

UN-LIKENESS

unalike preceding days
color again wash away grays
I've come and now I hope to stay
this must be light, must be the way

P G
———

do you remember peddling around all of Keene Valley?
how miserable, terrible, beautiful it was?
our legs screaming at us to stop
but we pushed each other on
until we found a break in the trees
a boulder stood firm
and we
leapt
into the river

that was one of my most favorite days

MOUNTAIN EDGE

standing at the base of this mountain
I realize how small we are

it's overwhelmingly significant
and utterly, ultimately, humbling

5:40 A.M.

5:40 a.m. the world sleeps
groggy I hear my alarm beeps
I leave my bedding in unmade heaps

I walk up the road in the morning mist
I notice the treetops the sun has kissed
I pray today there'll be nothing missed

I push through the door that creaks as it swings
I like to think it's a song the door sings
I hope I'll never forget these littlest things

KITCHEN

some days I was envious of those who worked on the water, in the sun, gulping in the fresh mountain air – this on the day the ovens cooked us in that hotbox kitchen along with the food inside its chambers; on the day the sun shone so purely, watery and thin, dappling through the window screens

and

some days I wondered why they chose me for this, if I was even capable of it – this on the day when the chicken wasn't pulled from the freezer in time for dinner service; on the day I under-baked the cornbread and it sat puddly on baking trays; on the day I killed the yeast with over warmed milk; on the day, on the day, on the day

and then also

every day I stood, washed in humble adoration, in awe of the essence of it, the culture of it, the privilege of it – this on the day when I learned how to time Wednesday's baking schedule just right; on the day when kitchen staff sat and ate together, just us; on the day when Big Cookie service went off without a hitch; on the day I took an after-breakfast rest in the kitchen office; on the day when we folded rags; we dropped a bakery container into the mixer; we deep cleaned the ovens, fryer, hood; we unloaded deliveries with roustabouts; we cut ice cream in the walk-in; we sang along to Disney classics; we gulped in long pulls of lemon water from our Nalgenes that stood as an army on the window sill; we prepped for buffets and canoe breakfast and breakfast in bed; we plated cake; we put way too much water in with the beans in the tilt skillet; we worked; we laughed; we laughed; we laughed; and this on the final day when we played "There Will Be Time," once more and Jake donned the mop head as a hat and we all gathered around the prep tables, voices loud enough we were sure they could be heard at the farthest reaches of camp

J N
—

If not for you,
I'm not sure I'd have made it through all those 6:00 a.m.s
If not for you,
I'm not sure I'd have left the day with my sanity intact
If not for you,
I'm not sure I'd have thrived the way I was able to
If not for you,
I'm not sure I'd have had nearly as much fun as we did

punkin muffins, sugar lips, post-breakfast naps, Disney songs, and
yes, even then, when you left the ovens full of mac and cheese
and I caught you leaping

If not for you,
I'd not be the same

CHILD

let live the child in you
the one that doesn't hide from rain
the one who doesn't know this pain
the one who has the world to gain

N W
———

be weird and be wild
have the heart of a child

be brave and be bold
have a heart made of gold

be goofy, be you
have a heart that is true

LEAN

if the music is good, and the words are true
lean in

S H

—

c'mon now
I can count on you
to smile when we're down
c'mon now
I can rely on you
to see silver 'round the cloud
c'mon now
I can trust in you
to be the quiet in a crowd
c'mon now
I can bank on you
to always be around

PINES

up away to the dancing pines floated the
secrets of our hearts and minds and
though we couldn't slow the time
the truth spilled out from our hearts and minds

all of us were safe up there amidst the
needles in the air and, if there's
something you can't bear, the pines have
ears and they want to hear

so our words departed reluctantly and we
watched them get caught in the trees
and then we fell upon our knees and
basked in little victories

because in open air it can be hard
to even reluctantly let go your guard, so if you
need to free your scars just look
to the trees in our front yard

L W

thank you for being unashamed and raw
for sharing all the things you saw
from up in the trees or down in the dirt
from all the joy to all the hurt
for being brave and having grit
and not being afraid to commit
you gave your all out on those ropes
and on the ground you founded hope

SENSES

I'm drunk on pine
as fresh water air fills my lungs
my skin gooseflesh
betrays summer sun

my veins pump oxygenated blood
hearts beat as lake waves lapping
my eyes shut tight
and fingers skim saplings

KE

—

it was never easy on you
the days they took their hold
you never let them break you down
you bent but didn't fold
you leaned into the nurture curve
and came out the other side
and all the while you stood tall
didn't drop or lose your pride
your worth was found where you belonged
and you shared with us your fight
we're honored to be next to you
and walk into the night

THE SHOP

steel beams sat somber in piles of ash
a memorial to the night of the flash
when combustion won in air so dry
and flames reached up to touch the sky
cause unknown caused walls to fall
and that one night we lost it all
morning gave way to smoking cinder
after evening tuned its way to tinder
we'll rise from ashes into something new
emerge victorious from this smoldering hue
buildings perish but closer we grow
we lean on each other and the truth that we know
together we come and fight through the fall
because even in the crumble we'll all stand tall

M K

you'd hear my broken heart
from one floor below
somehow you knew
and up you'd go

you'd find me in tears
my head on the floor
you'd comfort me there
and let all of me pour

you'd fight for my heart
and stand by my side
and because of your courage
I'd learn not to hide

TRYING TO SPEAK

you asked me the questions
I was afraid to answer

and you sat with me as
I fumbled
for
my words

SINK SANK SUNK

I sink beneath the surface
and the sound gives way to silence

RESURFACING

the summer was like
coming up for air
when you didn't even realize
you'd been living
underwater

MOORING

I surfaced at the dock, each breath a battle cry
the sun shone bright in a cloudless sky

my hand breaks through thick black tar
and I wonder how I've come so far

I run a hand along splintering wood
till it finds the thing I knew it would

steel protrudes and my hand it meets
I've found along the dock a cleat

limbs tied tight in ropes so soaked
I wonder how long until I choked

unravel, unravel, unravel the cord
tie to the cleat and now I'm moored

ABOVE THE ATMOSPHERE

I remember looking up at the stars
and seeing straight into Heaven

S R

—

it's funny how life
loops around on
itself
how things seem
to come
full circle
how people you know now
were pinpoints in your past
how our paths have crossed so long ago
but never really run parallel until now
and how in just a few months
unbeknownst to our present selves
we'll trade into each other's lives

BEAUTIFUL

the best of the beauty
is what was woven in between
the quietest times
that went unseen
I didn't know then how
much they'd come to mean
or how hard our hearts
would fight to lean

B B
———

you're a delicate force
a perfect blend of the two
soft sweet steel
always on cue

you hold people close
and would run into fire
and unlike the rest
you're a purifier

gentle on others
but strong in the storm
you're unshaken, unbroken
undeniably warm

we're thankful to know you
changed by your course
we hope to be like you
you delicate force

THE FIELDS

dewy grass beneath bare feet
sweat pools behind knees
together under summer heat
warm wind rattles pine trees

K R
——

simple and sweet
you don't fear what you might miss
because you know there's
nothing sweeter than this
true to yourself and
who made you so
it's toward your confidence
I hope to grow

LONG, WINDING, BACK ROADS

how do you describe what it's like to drive on these open roads, the way they curve and bend and give in to the delineations of the land? how do you describe the pine trees when there's too many to count creating a thick veil of deep green needles that interlock and weave? how do you describe the rush of cool air at 55 mph, your hand hanging out the window in a friction battle? how do you describe the painting in the sky, the one deep and rich in orange and red, a masterpiece of light and dark, one needing the other to survive? how do you describe the people inside it all, the ones who sing and laugh and shine?

BLED

the days
bled
into one another
in the same way
we did
each other

M K
———

your favorite thing was to pick on me
for being sad about the transience of this
but in some backward way
I knew that's how you cared for me

ICE CREAM CONES

the goosebumps on my legs rose and fell
in time with the late-night breeze
that seeped through the leaves
on the trees
but I didn't dare move—

this moment was too glorious to
abandon

T B

—

fierce as a fireball
spunky as a spring
speedy as a summer squall
poignant as a ping

HOT RAIN

hot rain fell heavy from the sky
we ran for shelter, a place to stay dry
but we laughed as we ran with the rain pouring down
and found our feet tied to this wet soggy ground

E B

---

you taught me
in the best and worst
way possible
how to love someone
who is totally
and fundamentally
different than me

and in the end I am thankful

IF ONLY WE LOOK

I've seen You in the wilderness
and from the mountaintops.
I've seen You in the rainbow sky
and in the clear raindrops.

I've felt You in the warm sunshine
and in the chilly nights.
I've seen You in the hail that storms
and in the morning light.

I've found You in the quiet
and in the loudest place.
I've seen You in the people here
and the way they show me grace.

You're everywhere we are;
honestly all around.
We sometimes just stop looking
until our knees hit ground.

THE BOATHOUSE

it's my favorite at night
when water laps in the slips
and floorboards creak and smell like
wet pine
and the yellow lights above glow like
beacons or clusters of fireflies
and the boats rock gently to sleep
after a hard day's work
when it's quiet enough to hear the
footfalls of your friends running
to catch up with you
and you
leap
leap
leap
from the dock and hoist
yourself up onto the Nautique platform
and others rock in the swing while you threaten to
toss them in too
and all of this
all of this
glowing in the beacons
and soundproofed by chirping crickets
and the water lapping

slapping
into the dock with
every
single
jump

TETHERED

I was tethered beyond all measure
to the One who gives me life
but the chain that held me on so tight
was lit with earthly light

SITTING IN THE LIVING ROOM

hot seat and bare feet
and digging underneath
shared stories and morning glories
and all that's in between

B B

it's rare to meet someone with a personality so big that it fills the space they're in. ricocheting from wall to wall. most people are too afraid, are too unsure, are too refined to be that big. but you let yourself fill, fill, fill up the room. it's refreshing for us all to be washed in the glory that is someone's unapologetic self.

THROUGH THE PANE

sun slanting
on denim skin
a knock at the door
says please let me in

wind seeping
through window panes
fire crackles leaving
pockmarked stains

trees swaying
just outside
one to the next
forever relied

darkness dancing
above us now
finding our voices
and learning to vow

quietly singing
everywhere
alone I sit
I sit and stare

dew arising
on the well-kept lawn
I try to move
but it's here that I'm drawn

R L
—

remember low-light nights?
the small pockets of quiet
when no one was home but us
when the sun had sunk
low below the horizon
and as the day faded into black
neither of us moved to turn on the lamps
we'd sit in the growing darkness
and tell each other the things
daylight would make us too scared
to say out loud
and we held on to one another
and hoped, against all odds,
that for even just a few more moments
no one would come home
and the sun wouldn't rise

MUNDANITY

barefoot on the tile floor
fingers pick at guitar chords
Thursday nights are for the chores
and soon they'll swing through broken doors

WHAT I'M THINKING
WHEN I WITHDRAW

I'm sitting in the middle
of an ordinary moment
but everything transcends it
I'm captivated in the silence of it
and I pray it never ends

W S
___

a dark horse
you have a rare and unique gift
of drawing out the best in people
patiently
lovingly
and encouraging them
to live as their best selves

ROAD TO CONE CABIN

remember driving down winding roads
streets lined in pine and windows down
music pumped through speakers loud
our collective voices rendering sound

skin on skin and toe to toe
how much farther left to go
air gets cool, sun goes low
our eyes twinkle, and they glow

she taps her feet on the vans rugged floor
she leans her head out the window's door
she sings too loud, her throat is sore
I remember then what I'm fighting for

A J
—

you're freeze pops and ice cream cups
you're free-range snacks and corgi pups
you're '50's night dances and rope swing rides
you're two shoulders on which I've cried
you're on the couch with all your friends
you're always there until the night ends
you're open ears and open heart
you're on our side right from the start
you're gentle and kind and pull us in
you're not afraid of your own sin
you're brave and bold and speak your mind
you're allowing our lives to intertwine
you're even-keeled wisdom which overflows
you're the one who always knows
you're a welcome home to us who stray
and your grace for us is new each day

THE POINT

sneak through the low trees
that line the wooded path
the one you'd never know is here
unless you'd come here in your past

walk until the road ends
when land gives way to lake
toe out to the water's edge
go and plant your stake

you're here now in the secret place
the place they shouldn't go
if you're wondering if you're home here
then this is how you'll know

beyond the borders lie the gifts
hidden treasure beyond the shore
all else makes it home for them
but these secrets make it yours

S S M

it's through some people
that we can so clearly see
Heaven
knowing you
is like finally correcting
my
blurred vision

THE THINGS THAT MATTER

to know and be known
to love and be loved
to invest and be invested in
to listen and be listened to
to pour and be poured into
to challenge and be challenged

SAPLINGS

thick bands of sap fall
from needles like rivers in
slow motion snaking
through veins
that emerge between
cracked bark

I watch and wait as if
by some magic of time
something magnificent
is going to happen here
before my bleary eyes

and I realize then that
some small magnificence has
unraveled before me
where something so critical
can move so slowly
and I realize it's time
I slow myself down

because even the slow,
the simple, the breathless
can be significant
and meaningful
and magnificent

LIKE SHOOTS

like shoots from the ground
we rose
into the people
we'd always
dreamt
of becoming

COME SEE

come and see the magic here
so you'll know why I never want to leave
come and meet the people here
so you'll know all I have to grieve

US ALL

it's not the single blade
that makes the lawn so
beautiful, but all of them
together

DREAMS

it was a culmination
of all the dreams I'd ever dreamt
and those I'd yet to have

EXISTENCE

here I've come to know
with profound clarity
and utter certainty
what a gift it is to even
exist

WHAT IT COMES DOWN TO

it's lake jumps and sandy feet
it's dancing to a solid beat
it's sunset's golden fingertip
it's jumping over the boat slip
it's snow one day and sun the next
it's not having enough service to text
it's more stars than you've ever seen
it's bending not to break but lean
it's early mornings and later nights
it's climbing up to higher heights
it's midnight pizza and ice cream cones
it's skipping rocks and throwing stones
it's laughter cramps and laughter tears
it's a culmination of our better years
it's volleyball games and scraped-up knees
it's letting go of your need to please
it's sparklers on the Fourth of July
it's being awestruck by the sky
it's phenomenal concerts and long drives
it's the best days of our lives
it's bike rides and getting caught in the rain
it's learning to push through the pain
it's meals eaten around the table
it's games made up involving a pretzel

it's burns and cuts and onion eyes
it's catching a glimpse of fireflies
it's reading good books and listening to good tunes
it's better than all of the other Junes
it's a horse head and yam pranks
it's understanding how to give thanks
it's a friendly face wherever you go
it's finding a balance between fast and slow
it's scooping cookies and rolling bread
it's making sure every mouth is fed
it's frisbee golf but not making par
it's learning to love exactly who you are
it's summer camp and oh my friend
it's the days you never want to end

PARTING

we left here as family
and scattered back across the country

THINGS YOU LEARN
FROM PARTING

It's late August, and summer feels hot and humid. Water sprays up over the edge of the Nautique, and I stick my hand over the hull as if out an open car window, letting pin-pricks of water pelt my palm. There's music playing loud through Gretchen's speakers, but it sounds muffled. I feel strange, but stranger still is how viscerally I notice how strange I feel even as this moment unravels. It's a gift I've become aware of these past few months, being able to appreciate a moment for all it's worth even before it ends. I also know that awareness isn't achieving, and even while I try to hang on to each moment as it happens, it still manages to ebb and flow away from me. I wish I was better at this. I snap my thoughts back to the boat I'm on and the people around me. It's hard to believe these people were complete strangers to me less than a season ago. I look around now and would trust any one of them with my life, with the deepest darkest points of brokenness inside of me. How did that happen so fast? They're smiling, all of them, singing, laughing. But there's a sadness there, too. An unspoken undercurrent of pain that seeps into curled lips and squinting eyes. It's the obvious that no one can address, we all look around its edges, pretending it isn't there for just a few more days, a few more hours. Sarah's got her camera out and is panning from face to face. And I smile a thanks to her from across the boat, knowing in her I've found the keeper of moments. A month from now that footage will lay itself across my computer screen, and I'll be transported back into this very scene.

Gretchen picks up speed as we carve deep ravines into the glass-like water. Emma or Tobin, I don't now remember which one, is racing alongside of us, our wakes serpentine, and we laugh and wave and snicker that we've edged ahead of them.

Our boats reach an inlet far, far away from our lake-side summer home. We pull into it becoming enclosed in pines that grow, somehow, from the depths of the rocky basin that bolsters this body of water. Roots mangle themselves in and around clumps of rock and their fruit skyrockets, pockets of green needles and leaves arching high overhead. We reach the middle of the clearing and tether our boats together. Even as it's happening, I know how symbolic it is, the action of tying two things together so that as they drift and rock, they drift and rock together. And now we are gathered. The sun is setting low and deep. In the distance, just outside the inlet, Tommy's Rock is backlit and silhouetted against the sky. As if it were a lapse, I watch as the sky fades to orange and red and yellow. Colors so rich and deep and I realize that there isn't any reason sunsets were given these colors other than for us to enjoy.

By the time we turn the keys over in their ignitions and head back to camp, the sky is deep blue, nearly purplish black. Gretchen makes her way back to Pelky Bay, Kat at the wheel, her hand gentle on the throttle. We don't know the next time we'll be back here. And we know we'll never be back here all together. We're in no hurry. We ease the motor and snake through the narrows. The air is chilly, and with my wet hair the breeze causes me to shiver. But I don't care. I'd sit here in these goosebumps forever. Soon we make the last turn toward camp, and that undercurrent of sadness threatens to betray itself in my eyes. I pull my sunglasses down off my head, cover my eyes, armor against the inevitable. I fight this moment. The lump in my throat suffocating me. I wonder if they can tell. I wonder who else feels it. I know they all do.

That's what the leaving is like. It's a battle you know you'll lose, but one you have to fight anyways. It's raw and visceral and undeniable. It's the realization that everything that has unfolded will live on only in caught memories. And you better hope you captured them well.

THE END(')S BEGINNING

it was easy in the beginning
not only because we had
what felt like so much time,
but because we didn't know
the way we'd come to love each other
in the end
and it was hard in the end
because as we looked up
and saw the days ahead of us shrinking
we looked around and saw
the way our hearts had tilted
toward one another

THE MOMENT OF THE END

you're always told you never know what you've got till it's gone. but I think I knew the whole time what I had. that didn't make it any easier to leave it all behind. we tell ourselves things to veil the pain, excuse it, justify it, minimize it. but in these waking hours I'm broken beyond repair. I sit wearing sunglasses inside, an attempt to hide the tears that swell and that threaten to break free from my eyes. I know they all know what's happening behind the lenses. they know me better than this. and yet I'm ashamed of the pain I feel. I slip between arms, from one to the next to the next until stillness comes. a wake of silence mourning their absence. the first threads of summer unraveling, unwinding, becoming undone.

IN SUM

and with me I'll take the moments that,
when woven together and cinched nice and tight,
become the entire sum of human existence

A COMMON SENTIMENT

every
single
time
without fail—
I felt my heart shredding

TO TRY AND HEAL

every goodbye
reopens a wound
I'd just barely got to close

SWEETNESS / BITTERNESS

It was sweet sitting with those who stayed
piled in our usual spots.
It was bitter looking all around
and seeing the places where you were not.

HANG TIGHT

I held on
even though my hands were shredding

THE FIRST NIGHT ALONE

when the lights go
out
and the room gets
dark
I couldn't see that you had gone.
but I could feel
emptiness all around me.

who knew the lack of something
could be so
suffocating?

FLEET

sometimes I wonder
if what made it so sweet
was knowing it would end

LUCID

this heart of mine is beating fast
hoping all of this will last
but knowing I can't hold the past

these hands of mine begin to shake
looking for some piece to take
fearful of the mistake I'll make

TYPE OF FRIENDS

these are the friends who would open up their home to you
the ones who'd keep food warm for you
the ones who'd drive all day for you
the ones who'd sit up at night with you
the ones who'd travel the world with you
the ones who'd sit and be still with you

POINTS OF ORIGIN

in the months that followed
I found that the best pieces of my life
all wind back to that summer
spent in the hollows of the mountains

HOME

I drove across the country and this place still feels like home

GEOGRAPHY OF HEARTACHE

I'd stitch the maps together
if it meant
shortening the distance
between us all again

REVIEW

it aches in the hollow of the memory
I close my eyes; it's all I see
time escapes just like a dream

I recall lake days spent fireside
I think of all the tears we cried
I know of all the love we tied

quiet nights and faster days
and all the things afraid to say
oh how I pleaded with you all to stay

like a film that plays inside my mind
I pause and watch and then rewind
to all the moments I could find

it aches in the hollow of the memory
I think of all the life we shared beneath those trees
and I'm thankful for this pain in me

J A
—

you're a mirage on the asphalt
an apparition of their mind
they run and run to get to you
but open air is all they find

but for the few, the lucky ones
of which we're counted in
you crystalized, taking shape
a solid form in skin

and from this paradox they can't escape
where they cling and can't let go
so we'll close our eyes as we leave this place
and cling to what we know

VAPOR

sometimes, now, it feels so far
like a vapor undefined
I reach out to grab hold of it
but it's only in my mind

PREPARATIONS

for months

and months

we prepared

and in a heartbeat it was over

OUTCOME

in the end
no matter the beginning or the middle
we'll all be welcomed home

IN US

the days between us and that summer are growing
inevitably,
irreversibly,
eternally,
but no matter how much time passes
no matter where we go
or when we see each other next
it will always
forever
be
a part of who we are

REWIND

I'd work until my hands hurt
survive on five hours of sleep
I'd dig with you through all life's dirt
I'd sit near while you weep
I'd do all the good and bad again
if it meant time would rewind

MONTHS TO COME

I started to wonder
in the reunion months
if he was right with what he said
that morning at the breakfast table

were those four months together
all we'd ever have?

DIFFERENTIATING

I don't remember the stories we told
or the things that made us cry
I don't remember the storms that came
or days with bright blue skies

I don't remember why we fought
or how we let it go
I don't remember being insecure
about the things I didn't know

but I do remember how you made me feel
alive and loved and good
I remember being welcomed home
and finally understood

THIS IS THE THING

the things that break us
are the things that make us
whole

ACKNOWLEDGMENTS

Thank you to Ariel So who edited this work with precision and care, to Asya Blue who turned my ramblings into a work of art, and to Alissa Zavalianos, who walked me through so much of this process. Without the expertise and vision of these three, you would not be holding this copy of *Saplings*.

Thank you to Kevin Mortiere for going with me on a whirlwind road trip to the ADKs to capture this amazing cover art and author photo. Thank you for indulging my whims and being spontaneous with me, cousin.

Thank you to my mom, my dad, my brother, my sister-in-law, and my entire family for being the only subscribers and readers of my blog and for encouraging me to keep writing. You are my biggest fans and I love you each dearly.

Thank you to Morgan Smith who encouraged me to dust off this manuscript that sat untouched for almost 3 years. You motivated me to be brave and bold. Thank you, too, to all of the camp staff; for the way you love kids, for the way you love Christ, and for making camp my home. It is from that hallowed ground this work is born.

Thank you to those of you who read this when it was binder clipped together on crinkled printer paper, and provided me with sticky notes of feedback and praise. I am forever grateful for your time and investment in me and this project.

And finally, thanks to Alex, Becca, Brennan, Eli, Jake, Jim, Kat, Kelsey, Kelsie, Lindsay, Maryn, Matt, Nate, Preston, Rachel, Sam,

Sarah, Schuyler, Tiffany, and Walker. For it is the 20 of you that bled through every single page of this book. Your friendships then and now are bright threads woven into the tapestry of my life and this book is, more than anything else, an ode to you and our summer in the pines.

ABOUT THE AUTHOR

Amanda Calabro is a writer and future elementary school teacher with New England roots who currently resides in Charlottesville, VA. *Saplings* is her first book.